The Human Life Cycle

Jennifer Prior

Consultant

Timothy Rasinski, Ph.D.
Kent State University
Lisa A. Leewood, C.S.T.
Erin P. Wayne, M.D.

Publishing Credits

Dona Herweck Rice, *Editor-in-Chief*

Robin Erickson, *Production Director*

Lee Aucoin, *Creative Director*

Conni Medina, M.A.Ed., *Editorial Director*

Jamey Acosta, *Editor*

Heidi Kellenberger, *Editor*

Lexa Hoang, *Designer*

Stephanie Reid, *Photo Editor*

Rachelle Cracchiolo, M.S.Ed., *Publisher*

Image Credits

Cover leungchopan/Shutterstock; Mike Tan C.T./Shutterstock; wong sze yuen/Shutterstock; p.3 Pete Pahham/Shutterstock; p.4 Petrenko Andriy/Shutterstock; p.5 top: N Photo/Shutterstock; p.5 left: Dr. Morley Read/Shutterstock; p.5 right: DJTaylor/Shutterstock; p.5 middle: Matej Ziak/Shutterstock; p.5 bottom: ex0rzist/Shutterstock; p.6 left to right: Gelpi/Shutterstock; Harm Kruyshaar/Shutterstock; michaeljung/Shutterstock; p.7 left to right: EDHAR/Shutterstock; Rob Marmion/Shutterstock; p.8 Ruta Saulyte-Laurinaviciene/Shutterstock; p.9 OJO Images/Photolibrary/Getty Images; p.10 Aliaksei Lasevich/Shutterstock; p.11 top to bottom: Punchstock; Lichtmeister/Shutterstock; p.12 JLBarranco/iStockphoto; p.13 bo1982/iStockphoto; p.14 StockLite/Shutterstock; p.15 Jenkedco/Shutterstock; p.16 BananaStock/Alamy; p.17 Stephanie Reid; p.18 Pete Pahham/Shutterstock; p.19 top to bottom: michaeljung/Shutterstock; Calvin Chan/Shutterstock; p.20 Anelina/Shutterstock; p.21 Rossario/Shutterstock; p.22-23 oliveromg/Shutterstock; p.24 Alamy; p.25 Monkey Business Images/Shutterstock; p.26 Eyewire/Punchstock; p.27 Brand X Pictures/Punchstock; p.28 Monkey Business Images/Shutterstock; p.29 top to bottom: Monkey Business Images/Shutterstock; ClickPop/Shutterstock; p.32 Beata Becla/Shutterstock; back cover Harm Kruyshaar/Shutterstock

Based on writing from *TIME For Kids*.

TIME For Kids and the *TIME For Kids* logo are registered trademarks of TIME Inc. Used under license.

Teacher Created Materials

5301 Oceanus Drive
Huntington Beach, CA 92649-1030
http://www.tcmpub.com

ISBN 978-1-4333-3678-2

© 2012 Teacher Created Materials, Inc.
Printed in China
Nordica.122018.CA21801489

Table of Contents

The Life Cycle of Change

Most of us know about the **life cycles** of butterflies and frogs. They begin as eggs and then change and grow throughout their lives. But have you thought about the life cycle of a human being?

Newborn babies are just beginning their life cycles.

Life Cycle of a Frog

adult frog

eggs

tadpole

froglet

adult stinkbug
with hatchlings
and eggs

People change and grow from the time they are born until the time they die. They keep learning, too. People develop wonderful **abilities** as they grow.

People grow from infancy to childhood, to adolescence, to adulthood, and finally to old age.

Think about all the things you can do today. Could you do those things just a few years ago?

Infants often learn about the world around them by putting things in their mouths.

How Big?

Babies are tiny, but they don't all weigh the same when they are born. Newborn babies usually weigh between 5 and 11 pounds at birth. But some babies are as small as one pound at birth and have survived. The largest baby ever born, according to the *Guinness Book of World Records*, was 24 pounds! That's the size of three or four average babies!

Infancy

We all begin as babies. This is called **infancy**. Infancy is a time of fast growth and change in a short period of time.

One to Four Months

At first, babies, or **infants**, are helpless. They are very small, and they need 15 to 18 hours of sleep each day. Over time, they learn to hold their heads up and roll over.

Young babies don't have good eyesight, but their senses of smell, hearing, and taste are very good. What do babies do when they grab toys? They put them in their mouths. This is the best way they have to explore their world.

As their eyesight develops, young babies begin to identify different faces. They can tell the differences between colors and patterns. They begin to imitate people's **expressions**. They recognize the voices of their **caregivers**. And they communicate, mostly through crying.

Eyesight

Young babies are best able to see things that are 6 to 12 inches away from them.

Four to Eight Months

Between the ages of four and eight months, some babies get their first teeth. Many learn to sit up and crawl. They laugh when playing with others and make eye contact with them. Some use hand motions and sounds to communicate.

At this age, most babies are very attached to their mothers or **primary** caregivers. They are usually afraid of strangers.

You or Me?

When babies are very young, they don't understand that other people are separate from them. They think that everything is a part of them. Sometime during their infancy, they begin to understand that Mom, Dad, and everyone else are separate people. This is why they sometimes get frightened when their parents are away. They don't like the idea of being separated from them.

Babies need parents to care for them. Otherwise, they could not survive in the world.

Eight to Twelve Months

By the time babies reach 8 to 12 months old, they may learn to stand. Some can even walk. But most babies at this age still enjoy crawling. They eat most foods, and some can drink from a cup.

At this age, some babies can name many people, animals, toys, and body parts, too. They can even make animal sounds. They begin to take turns when talking to people. Most babies like to play simple games such as peek-a-boo.

Humor

This is the age when babies really start to develop a sense of humor. Peek-a-boo is very funny to them. The sudden appearance of a friendly face can make them laugh again and again.

Between 9 and 18 months of age, babies learn to walk.

Toddlers enjoy being able to get around by themselves to explore their worlds.

What Is It?

To toddle is to walk in a somewhat unsteady manner. That is why new walkers are called *toddlers*, because they toddle and often fall when they walk.

One to Two Years

At this age, babies are called **toddlers**. Most are able to move around a lot, walking and climbing. Many are also very **social**. This means that they like to be around people. They wave goodbye and speak more and more words. Some toddlers can follow simple directions. They recognize the people they know in photos. They begin to enjoy being read to.

As children near the age of two, they can do quite a lot. Many know 200–300 words and begin to speak in short sentences. They also begin to develop opinions about things. You may often hear a toddler say, "No" and "Mine."

Children this age enjoy someone reading them a story. Of course, most people continue to enjoy stories all their lives.

Childhood

Childhood is separated into two stages: the preschool years and the school-aged years.

Preschool Years

Between the ages of two and five, children are in the preschool stage. Many begin to draw and count. They learn to cut with scissors, to identify colors and shapes, and to identify letters of the alphabet. They learn to dress themselves. They feed themselves, too, using utensils such as forks, knives, and spoons.

Imagine That!

A child's imagination really is very active during this time. This is a great age for playing dress-up. Young children like to imagine themselves doing all kinds of things. When you were a little boy or girl, what did you like to imagine?

The preschool years are very creative.

Children speak quite well at this stage. They like to play with other children for short periods of time. Most of the time, they enjoy playing alone but near other children. As they near the age of five, they become better able to share with their friends. They enjoy thinking of themselves as grown-ups, and they like to tell others about the things they are able to do.

School-Aged Years

School-aged children can do a lot of things. They also learn new things every day. Just think of something you recently learned to do.

Children at this age usually learn to read. They are also very social and active. They like to run, play, solve puzzles, make crafts, and build things. Some children learn to play sports and instruments.

Girls usually like to play with girls. Boys usually like to play with boys. They often form organized groups or clubs with their friends. Does that sound like you?

Boys and Girls

Before going to school, children don't spend a lot of time thinking about being a boy or a girl. This is the age when that usually becomes more important to children. They find more and more ways to enjoy being a boy or a girl.

You and Food

Don't be surprised if you eat more and more as you grow. Your body needs all the nutrients it can get. It is growing and changing fast. That's why healthy food is very important. Remember to eat the healthiest food you can. Healthy food will help you to grow taller and stronger with more energy.

In later childhood, friends become very important. Most children want to fit in. They usually like to help their teachers and parents with real-life tasks. They also enjoy helping younger children. As they age, they begin to feel like adults. They believe they can take care of themselves. Have you ever felt that way? Girls usually grow faster than boys during this time. But don't worry, the boys catch up in time.

You and Your Brain

Have you noticed that as you get older, you start to think in different ways? New things are becoming important to you. You understand things differently than you did when you were younger. This is because while your body grows in size, the abilities of your brain grow as well. Part of growing up is a developing and changing mind. Growing up means that you are thinking more and more for yourself. Good for you!

Adolescence

Adolescence is also known as the *teenage years*. This can be a tough but exciting time for kids. So many changes are happening in their bodies. Kids at this age can feel unsure of themselves. Sometimes they don't feel normal. They are often **moody**. That means that one minute they are happy and the next minute they are upset. Do you know any teenagers who act that way?

Most teenagers are able to express themselves as adults, but they seek out role models to imitate. It is important that they find role models who are worth looking up to. Adolescents usually wonder about themselves. They try to figure out who they are and how they fit into the world.

Making Choices

One of the most challenging things about being an adolescent is the choices you must make. As an adolescent, you begin to have much more freedom than you had as a child. With freedom comes **responsibility**. You must be responsible for making good choices. It is up to you to pick kind and supportive friends, to do your best in school, to help at home, and to be a good friend yourself. Sometimes when people have a lot of freedom, they forget that they have important responsibilities as well.

During adolescence, teenagers try new activities and make new friends. They spend time trying to figure out who they are and what is important to them.

Adulthood

Adulthood happens when a person's body is fully grown and his or her mind is **mature** enough to take on adult responsibilities and work. When you reach adulthood, there are even more responsibilities than those that begin to develop in adolescence. During their adulthoods, people often get married and begin to have children. They find careers and work hard to take care of their families. Adults usually place great importance on their family life and their jobs. In fact, experts say that adults feel a need to care for their families just as much as their families need their care. That works out great for everyone, doesn't it?

When You Grow Up

Do you sometimes imagine what life will be like when you are grown? What do you think you will be doing? What do you hope to achieve?

One of the best things about being an adult is loving and caring for your family.

Old Age

Eventually, if people are lucky, they grow to old age. Do you have a grandparent or an older family friend? You know that changes happen to the body as people age. Their hair turns gray or white, their skin wrinkles, and they begin to slow down a bit.

Often, older people spend time looking back on their lives. They think about their families and the things they did to make a difference. Many people say that as they get older, they become more grateful for their families. They realize that their families and their relationships with people are the most important things in their lives.

Don't Miss Out!

If you have some older people in your life, be sure to tell them how important they are to you. Ask them to tell you some stories about their lives, especially about when they were your age. They are sure to have many good stories to tell!

Old age can be a time of great fun and freedom if a person does what it takes to stay fit and healthy.

Staying Healthy as We Age

Some people believe that old age means a lot of illness, but this isn't necessarily true. People can take good care of their bodies all their lives with good food, exercise, positive thoughts, and happy relationships. If they do, they will probably enjoy old age with good health and lots of energy.

Time Marches On

The life cycle from birth to old age is an amazing process. It is filled with many changes at each stage along the way. As a child, you have much to look forward to, and as an adult, you can look back on many wonderful experiences. But as long as a person is living, he or she is constantly growing and changing. No matter how old you are, there is more beautiful life ahead of you!

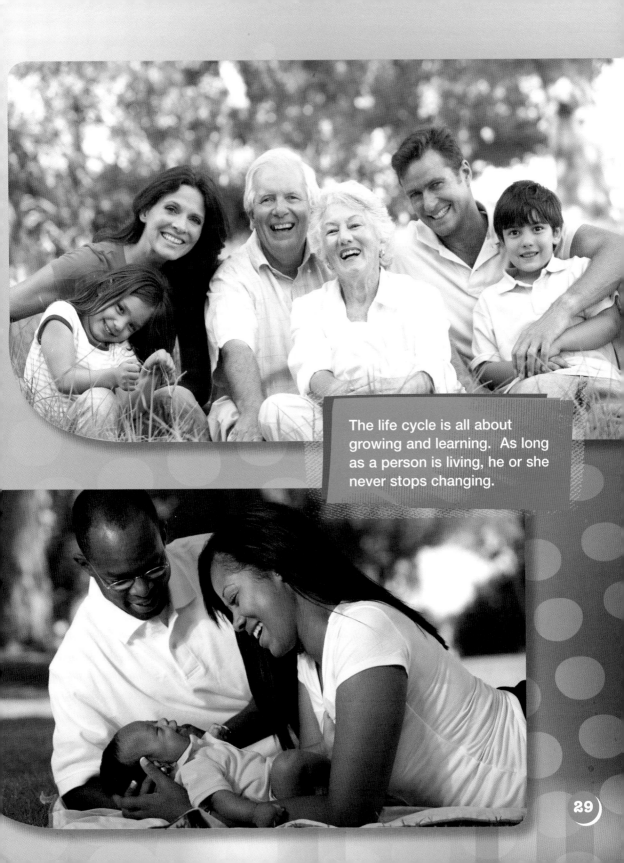

The life cycle is all about growing and learning. As long as a person is living, he or she never stops changing.

Glossary

abilities—the qualities of being able to do things

adolescence—the time of life between childhood and adulthood, usually thought of as the teenage years

adulthood—the time of life of a fully grown person

caregivers—people who take care of other people

childhood—the state of being a child, usually thought of as between the ages of about 2 and 12

expressions—movements of the face that show different feelings such as happiness, sadness, and anger

infancy—the beginning stage of human life; babyhood

infants—young babies

life cycles—the stages in the lives of living things

mature—grow into adult level

moody—emotional, with a variety of changing feelings

primary—the number one or most important

responsibility—a duty or obligation

social—able to get along well with others

toddlers—young children about one or two years old who, as new walkers, are a bit unsteady when walking and often fall

Index

About the Author

Jennifer Prior is a professor and a writer. She has written a wide range of books for Teacher Created Materials. Jennifer lives in Flagstaff, Arizona, with her husband and four pets.